MOROCCO 2016 HUMAN RIGHTS REPORT

EXECUTIVE SUMMARY

Morocco is a constitutional monarchy under which ultimate authority rests with King Mohammed VI, who presides over the Council of Ministers. The king may dismiss ministers, dissolve parliament and call for new elections, or rule by decree. The king shares executive authority with the head of government (prime minister), whom he must appoint from the political party with the most seats in parliament, and approves members of the government nominated by the prime minister. International and domestic observers judged the October 7 parliamentary elections credible and relatively free from irregularities. The Islamist-leaning ruling party, Party of Justice and Development (PJD), again won a plurality of seats in the elections. As mandated by the constitution, immediately following the October 7 elections, the king chose the PJD to lead the governing coalition and nominated PJD Secretary General Abdelilah Benkirane to serve again as head of government. During the year the government continued to implement its "advanced regionalization" plan, allowing local bodies elected in 2015 to exercise increased budgetary and decision-making powers.

Civilian authorities at times did not maintain effective control over security forces.

The most significant continuing human rights problems were corruption, discrimination against women, and disregard for the rule of law by security forces.

A variety of sources reported other human rights problems. These included Security forces occasionally committing human rights abuses, including reports of mistreatment in detention. While prison and detention center conditions improved during the year, in some instances, they still did not meet international standards. Pretrial detention conditions were especially a problem due to overcrowding, and detention periods were often prolonged. The judiciary lacked full independence, and sometimes denied defendants the right to a fair public trial. Domestic and international nongovernmental organizations (NGOs) asserted there were political prisoners, although the government asserted that these individuals were charged with criminal offenses. The government abridged civil liberties by infringing on freedom of speech and press, including by harassing and arresting print and internet journalists for reporting or commenting on issues sensitive to the government. The government also limited freedom of assembly and association and restricted the right to practice one's religion. The power of the elected government was limited on certain national policy issues. The government placed

restrictions on domestic and international human rights organizations, depending on its evaluation of the political orientation of the organization and the sensitivity of the issues. Trafficking in persons and child labor continued to occur, particularly in the informal sector.

There were few examples of investigations or prosecutions of abuse or corruption by officials, whether in the security services or elsewhere in the government, which contributed to the widespread perception of impunity.

Section 1. Respect for the Integrity of the Person, Including Freedom from:

a. Arbitrary Deprivation of Life and other Unlawful or Politically Motivated Killings

There were no reports that the government or its agents committed arbitrary or unlawful killings.

b. Disappearance

There were no reported cases of politically motivated disappearance during the year.

Regarding unresolved cases of disappearance dating to the 1970s and 1980s, the National Council on Human Rights (CNDH), a publicly funded national human rights institution that operates independently, continued to investigate claims of enforced and involuntary disappearance from previous years. When warranted the CNDH recommended reparations in the form of money, health care, employment, or vocational training to victims (or victims' families) of forced disappearance. In the last several years, the government shifted its focus from outstanding and new individual claims to community reparation projects. The CNDH continued to receive and investigate reparation claims throughout the year. According to the CNDH, there were six cases unresolved as of October and four cases presented by families before the courts. (For more information on reparation claims in Western Sahara, see the Department of State's annual *Country Reports on Human Rights* for Western Sahara.)

c. Torture and Other Cruel, Inhuman, or Degrading Treatment or Punishment

The constitution and the law prohibit such practices, and the government denied it used torture. The law defines torture and stipulates that all government officials or members of security forces who "make use of violence against others without legitimate motive, or incite others to do the same, during the course of their duties shall be punished in accordance with the seriousness of the violence." A 2006 amendment to the law provides a legal definition of torture in addition to setting punishments for instances of torture according to their severity. The government also enacted measures designed to eliminate torture. For example, in November 2014 the government deposited its ratification of the Optional Protocol to the Convention against Torture with the United Nations--with the CNDH filling the role of investigative organ for the prevention of torture. Reports of torture have declined over the last several years, although government institutions and NGOs such as Amnesty International (AI) and Human Rights Watch (HRW) continued to receive reports about the mistreatment of individuals in official custody. The UN Human Rights Committee monitoring implementation of the International Covenant on Civil and Political Rights final observations on the country's sixth periodic report issued December 1 noted that the government has taken steps to combat torture and mistreatment and that there was a "marked reduction" in such practices since its 2004 report. The committee remained concerned by continued allegations of torture and mistreatment by government agents, in particular on persons suspected of terrorism or threats to national security or territorial integrity.

Reporting in previous years alleged more frequent use of torture. A May 2015 report by AI claimed that between 2010 and 2014, security forces routinely inflicted beatings, asphyxiation, stress positions, simulated drowning, and psychological and sexual violence to "extract confessions to crimes, silence activists, and crush dissent." Since the AI interviews, the government has undertaken reform efforts, including widespread human rights training for security and justice sector officials. In June 2015 Minister of Justice Mustapha Ramid publicly announced that torture would not be tolerated, and that any public official implicated in torture would face imprisonment.

In the event of an accusation of torture, the law requires judges to refer a detainee to a forensic medical expert when the detainee or lawyer requests it or if judges notice suspicious physical marks on a detainee. The UN Working Group on Arbitrary Detention, human rights NGOs, and media documented cases of authorities' failure to implement provisions of the antitorture law, including failure to conduct medical examinations when detainees allege torture. Following the recommendations of the Special Rapporteur for Torture's 2013 report, the Ministries of Justice, Prison Administration, and National Police each issued notices to their officials to respect the prohibition against maltreatment and torture, reminding them of the obligation to conduct medical examinations in all cases where there are allegations or suspicions of torture. Since January 2015 the Ministry of Justice has organized a series of human rights trainings for judges, including on the prevention of torture. In June the Ministry of Justice issued a notice to courts instructing them to implement the recommendation from the Special Rapporteur to visit local jail and detention facilities at least twice per month.

During the year the CNDH reported that it received 34 complaints alleging torture in internationally recognized Morocco, a 56 percent decrease from the previous year. After investigating all 34 allegations, the CNDH substantiated four allegations, one instance each in Khouribga, Tetouan, Toulal 2, and Sale 1 prisons. The CNDH referred one case (Sale 1) to the public prosecutor's office, while two other cases were opened by detainees' lawyers (Khouribga and Tetouan). In the case of Toulal 2, the CNDH was unable to obtain sufficient evidence to refer the case to the prosecutor and, instead, submitted recommendations to the Prison Administration (DGAPR). Regarding the four cases referred by the CNDH to the public prosecutor in 2015, the cases remained in the judicial system at year's end. The DGAPR indicated that it referred one prison official to the judicial system for causing injury to a detainee during the year.

In 2015 the government investigated 42 public officials for torture or abuse. Of those officials 19 remained under investigation, three cases before the courts, and 20 completed the judicial process at year's end. For example, on June 7, courts sentenced five gendarmes to sentences between five and 10 years for murder and falsifying evidence in relation to the death of an individual in custody in September 2015. According to a Ministry of Interior statement regarding the death, which was shared with media, they abused the individual during his arrest, and he died during transfer to a hospital. Three prison officials who were referred to the courts in September 2015 for abuse of detainees received sentences of four months' detention and fines of 500 dirhams ($50.20) in March. They have appealed the decision. The government prosecuted 14 police officers in relation to the death of a detainee in custody in August 2015. On November 30, eight of the officials were convicted of torture and "use of violence against a detainee in a fragile psychological state resulting in unintentional death," while a ninth official was convicted of failure to report a felony. Five other officers were acquitted. The nine received sentences ranging from one to 10 years in addition to fines of 150,000 dirhams ($15,625) each.

During the year, according to United Nations data, there were six allegations of sexual exploitation and abuse made against Moroccan peacekeepers deployed to UN peacekeeping operations in the Central African Republic and the Democratic Republic of the Congo. Three of the alleged incidents occurred during the year, one in 2015, and two in 2014. According to the United Nations, five of these allegations were being investigated jointly by the United Nations and the government, and one was pending investigation. Investigations were completed on four allegations reported in previous years. One claim of sexual abuse was substantiated, and three abuse and exploitation claims were determined to be unsubstantiated allegations after joint UN-government investigations.

Prison and Detention Center Conditions

Prison conditions improved during the year, but in some cases did not meet international standards.

<u>Physical Conditions</u>: The Moroccan Observatory of Prisons continued to report that some prisons were overcrowded and failed to meet local and international standards. The DGAPR indicated that overcrowding had decreased with the opening of 26 new prisons in the past three years, including three during the year. DGAPR statistics indicate that the average space allocated per detainee increased from 18.8 square feet in 2015 to 20.3 square feet during the year, due to the opening of the new prisons. These 26 new prisons represent approximately 35 percent of the country's prisons, and were built to international standards. In the new prisons, pretrial detainees and convicted prisoners were held separately. As construction on each new prison was completed, older prisons were closed, and inmates were moved to the new locations. Older prisons remained overcrowded, resulting in authorities frequently holding pretrial detainees and convicted prisoners together. According to government sources and NGOs, prison overcrowding was due in large part to an underutilized system of bail or provisional release, a severe backlog in cases, and lack of judicial discretion to reduce the length of prison sentences for specific crimes. Government sources stated that a further complication was that administrative requirements prevented prison authorities from transferring individuals in pretrial detention to facilities outside the jurisdiction where their trials were to take place. As of September authorities released 45,071 individuals on bail. In 2015 authorities released 65,065 individuals on bail.

The law provides for the separation of minors. In all prisons, officials identify youthful offenders into two categories, and they are held separately from other categories: minors under 18, and youthful offenders from 18 to 20 years old. Authorities held a number of minors with adults, particularly in pretrial detention in ordinary prisons and police stations, due to shortage of juvenile prison facilities. DGAPR has four dedicated juvenile "centers for reform and education," but maintains separate, dedicated youth detention areas in all prisons for minors. As of September 30, minors under 18 years old represented 2.7 percent of the overall prison population (2,131 minors of a prison population of 78,875). The government reported that in cases where a juvenile court judge ruled that their detention was necessary, minors less than 14 years old were detained separately from minors 15 to 18 years old. HRW stated that in one case involving two minors arrested October 27 on suspicion of same-sex sexual conduct, authorities held the minors with adult prisoners, and the minors allegedly were subjected to threats and harassment.

While there was less overcrowding in the women's sections of facilities, according to a CNDH study early this year, conditions in women's sections often did not meet the 2010 United Nations Rules for the Treatment of Women Prisoners and Noncustodial Measures for Women Offenders. The study noted that health facilities were generally located in the men's sections, restricting access for female prisoners, and that vocational training opportunities were limited for women. The study also noted that female prisoners faced discrimination from staff, including medical staff, on the basis of their gender. As of September 30, there were 1,815 female prisoners, in a total population of 78,875 (2.3 percent of prison population), according to DGAPR data.

Local NGOs asserted that prison facilities did not provide adequate access to health care and did not accommodate the needs of prisoners with disabilities, although government sources stated that each prisoner received an average of six consultations with a medical professional per year and that all care was provided free of charge. According to DGAPR 2015 statistics, there was one doctor for every 675 inmates and one nurse for every 135 inmates. The government reported that 129 inmates died during the year, 19 in the prisons and 110 in a hospital. Of these deaths, 124 were from natural causes or medical conditions, four were from suicide, and one from accidental electrocution. Local human rights NGOs could not confirm these numbers.

On April 15, activist Brahim Saika died days after reporting to the prosecutor's office, and his family claimed that officers at the Guelmim police station had mistreated him following his April 1 arrest and that he had begun a hunger strike in protest. Saika reportedly was arrested as he sought to join a protest and was charged with insulting and assaulting police officers and insulting a public institution.

The prosecutor ordered an investigation by the judicial police to determine the conditions and circumstances of Saika's death, in addition to an autopsy, which established the cause of death as natural and due to a microbial infection, noting that the hunger strike may have contributed to the death. The medical exam revealed no traces of torture or mistreatment on Saika's body. The judicial police of the Royal Gendarmerie and the National Police conducted separate investigations before determining that there was no torture committed, and the death was a medical event unrelated to torture or abuse. CNDH was also notified of the complaint and conducted an investigation, and found the claims to be unsubstantiated. Following a request of the family lawyers, however, another autopsy took place on April 22, concluding that the death was "secondary to a septic infection in the context of hunger strike." There was no independent autopsy completed despite the family's request.

According to information provided by the CNDH, in response to domestic and international interest in the case, the prosecutor ordered an investigation by the judicial police to determine the conditions and circumstances of death, in addition to an autopsy, which established the cause of death as natural and due to a microbial infection.

DGAPR provides food to inmates at no cost, and since 2015 a private company provided higher quality options than were previously available. Prison commissaries stock fresh fruit and vegetables for purchase, and families were permitted to bring food baskets once per week. NGOs frequently cited cases where prisoners protested the conditions of their detention with hunger strikes, According to AI prisoners launched hunger strikes to protest harsh conditions, including poor hygiene and sanitation, inadequate nutrition and healthcare, severe overcrowding, and detention far from their families, as well as limited visiting rights and access to education.

Some human rights activists have asserted the prison administration reserved harsher treatment for Islamists who challenged the king's religious authority and those accused of "questioning the territorial integrity of the country." The UN special rapporteur's 2013 report on torture, however, stated, "The majority of the victims examined in the prisons visited denied ever being subjected to any kind of torture or degrading treatment inside prison establishments. Also, the allegations received usually pointed to a small number of staff committing these violations--

the majority of the penitentiary staff is not involved in such violations." There have been no visits or reports from the rapporteur since 2013. DGAPR denied that any prisoners received differential treatment, and asserts that all prisoners were treated equally in accordance with the Prison Act.

Administration: Prison administration recordkeeping was adequate. Authorities did not implement alternatives to imprisonment for nonviolent offenders.

While authorities generally permitted relatives and friends to visit prisoners, there were reports that the authorities denied visiting privileges in some instances.

The CNDH and DGAPR investigated allegations of inhuman conditions. The CNDH and the DGAPR effectively served the function of an ombudsman, and a system of "letterboxes" continued to operate in prisons to facilitate prisoners' right to submit complaints regarding their imprisonment. Detainees could submit complaints without censorship. Complaints were brought to the DGAPR Delegate General's Office for processing, as well as to the CNDH.

Independent Monitoring: The government permitted some NGOs with a human rights mandate to conduct unaccompanied monitoring visits. Government policy permitted NGOs that provided social, educational, or religious services to prisoners to enter prison facilities, and prison authorities reported that NGOs conducted 673 prison visits during the first nine months of the year, in addition to 127 regular prison monitoring visits conducted by the CNDH. According to DGAPR statistics, parliamentarians, media, and religious, judicial, and other government authorities conducted more than 3,000 prison visits during the year.

Improvements: To alleviate overcrowding government authorities reported opening three new detention facilities during the year. The government reported increasing the number of vocational and educational training programs it administers in prisons. The Mohammed VI Foundation for the Reinsertion of Prisoners provided educational and professional training to inmates on the verge of release, providing job-skills training, literacy, and education through university level.

d. Arbitrary Arrest or Detention

The constitution prohibits arbitrary arrest and detention. Observers indicated that police did not always respect these provisions or consistently observe due process. According to local NGOs and associations, police sometimes arrested persons without warrants, held detainees beyond the statutory deadline to charge them, and failed to identify themselves when making arrests.

Role of the Police and Security Apparatus

The security apparatus includes several police and paramilitary organizations with overlapping authority. The National Police (Direction Generale de la Surete Nationale--DGSN) manages internal law enforcement and reports to the Ministry of Interior. The Auxiliary Forces also report to the Ministry of Interior and support gendarmes and police. The Royal Gendarmerie, which reports to the Administration of National Defense, is responsible for law enforcement in rural regions and on national highways. The judicial police (investigative) branches of both the Royal Gendarmerie and the National Police report to the royal prosecutor and have the power to arrest individuals. The Department of Royal Security is a branch of the National Police that provides protection for the king and royal family members. The Directorate General of Territorial Surveillance (Direction Generale de la Surveillance Territoriale--DGST) has intelligence gathering responsibilities, without arrest powers, and reports to the Ministry of Interior.

Civilian authorities failed at times to maintain effective control over the security forces, and there were reports of abuses and impunity. Systemic and pervasive corruption undermined law enforcement and the effectiveness of the judicial system.

Impunity was widespread in the absence of effective mechanisms to investigate and punish abuse and corruption. International and domestic human rights organizations claimed that authorities dismissed many complaints of abuse and relied only on police versions of events.

Authorities investigated some low-level incidents of alleged abuse and corruption. The judicial police investigate allegations, including those against security forces, and advise the court of their findings. While authorities suspended some individuals accused of human rights abuses, they did not systematically prosecute or sentence security personnel who committed human rights abuses. Cases often languished in the investigatory or trial phases. In 2015 courts investigated and found guilty of corruption 16 members of the Royal Gendarmerie who were sentenced to prison terms and fines, while 14 others were acquitted and returned to duty. As of October courts have investigated 21 members of the Gendarmerie for corruption, with one conviction resulting in a two-month prison sentence, two acquittals, and 18 were in the judicial process.

Arrest Procedures and Treatment of Detainees

Police may arrest an individual after a general prosecutor issues an oral or written warrant. The law provides for access to a lawyer in the first 24 hours after arrest in ordinary criminal cases, but authorities did not consistently respect that provision. The law permits authorities to deny defendants' access to counsel or family members during the initial 96 hours of detention under terrorism-related laws or during the initial 24 hours of detention for other charges, with an optional extension of 12 hours with the approval of the Prosecutor's Office. Reports of abuse generally referred to these initial detention periods, when police interrogated detainees.

The law states "in the case of a flagrant offense, the Judicial Police Officer has the right to keep the suspect in detention for 48 hours. If strong and corroborated evidence is raised against this person, [the officer] can keep them in custody for a maximum of three days with the written authorization of the prosecutor." For normal crimes authorities can extend this 48-hour period twice, for up to six days in detention. Under terrorism-related laws, a prosecutor may renew the initial detention by written authorization for a total detention time of 12 days. According to the Antiterrorism Act, there is no right to a lawyer during this time except for a half-hour monitored visit at the midpoint of the 12-day period. Observers widely perceived the 2015 law on counterterrorism as consistent with international standards.

NGO sources stated that some judges were reticent to use alternative sentences permitted under the law, such as provisional release. The law does not require written authorization for release from detention. In some instances judges released defendants on their own recognizance. A bail system exists; the deposit may be in the form of property or as a sum of money paid to court in an effort to persuade the judge to release a suspect. The amount of the deposit is left to the discretion of the judge, who decides the amount of the deposit depending on the offense. Bail may be requested at any time before the judgment. According to the law, all defendants have the right to attorneys; if a defendant cannot afford private counsel, authorities must provide a court-appointed attorney when the criminal penalty exceeds five years in prison. Authorities did not always provide effective counsel.

In ordinary criminal cases, the law requires police to notify a detainee's next of kin of the arrest immediately after the above-mentioned period of incommunicado detention, unless arresting authorities applied for and received an extension from a magistrate. Police did not consistently abide by this provision. Because authorities sometimes delayed notifying the family, authorities did not inform lawyers promptly of the date of arrest, and they were not able to monitor compliance with detention limits and treatment of the detainee. Under a separate military code, military authorities may detain members of the military without a warrant or public trial.

Arbitrary Arrest: Security forces often arrested groups of individuals, took them to a police station, questioned them for several hours, and released them without charge. Under the penal code, any public official who orders an arbitrary detention is punishable by demotion and, if it is done in a private interest, by imprisonment of 10 years to life. An official who neglects to refer a claim or observation of arbitrary or illegal detention to his superiors is punishable by demotion. There was no available information that these provisions were applied this year.

While in previous years, authorities have been accused of arresting undocumented migrants, detaining them, and escorting them to the borders or otherwise expelling them without an opportunity to exercise their legal rights, UNCHR and NGOs noted that there were no such reports this year.

Pretrial Detention: Although the government claimed that authorities generally brought accused persons to trial within two months, prosecutors may request as many as five additional two-month extensions of pretrial detention. Pretrial detentions can last as long as one year, and there were reports that authorities routinely held detainees beyond the one-year limit. Government officials attributed these delays to the large backlog of cases in the justice system. The Foreign Ministry stated that a variety of factors contributed to this backlog: a lack of resources devoted to the justice system, both human and infrastructure; the lack of plea bargaining as an option for prosecutors, lengthening the amount of time to process cases on average; and the scant use of mediation and other out-of-court settlement mechanisms allowed by law. The government reported that as of September 30, 43.1 percent of detainees were in pretrial detention. In some cases detainees received a sentence shorter than the time they spent in pretrial detention.

Detainee's Ability to Challenge Lawfulness of Detention before a Court: The constitution states that "No one may be detained, arrested, prosecuted, or sentenced outside of the cases and forms prescribed by the law," and gives the right to compensation in cases of judicial error. Individuals have the right to challenge the legal basis or arbitrary nature of their detention and request compensation by submitting a complaint to the court. If the complaint is unsubstantiated, the accused has the right to file for damages against the accuser.

<u>Amnesty</u>: The king continued to exercise his ability to grant pardons to those convicted of crimes. The decision-making process for granting royal pardons was not publicly available; however, the committee took into account health, social situation, participation in rehabilitation and reintegration programs, and degree of behavioral improvement when making its decisions. Certain individuals were not eligible for pardons, including those who had previously benefitted from a pardon and those convicted of certain serious crimes. Individuals who benefitted from pardons were not subject to arbitrary re-arrest during the year.

e. Denial of Fair Public Trial

The constitution provides for an independent judiciary, and, in previous years, government officials, NGOs, and lawyers widely acknowledged that corruption and extrajudicial influence weakened judicial independence. During the year the government established the Supreme Judicial Council, a new government body that provides authority for judges to manage the courts and judicial affairs, designed to supplant management by the Ministry of Justice. While the government stated its aim of creating the council was to improve judicial independence, the council was not fully functional at year's end, and its effect on judicial independence was not clear. The outcomes of trials in which the government had a strong political stake, such as those touching on Islam as it related to political life and national security, the monarchy, and the Western Sahara, appeared predetermined.

In February a disciplinary panel of the Higher Judicial Council dismissed Judge Mohamed El-Haini, following allegations referred by the Ministry of Justice that he had "violated the duty of discretion" and "expressed opinions of a political nature." The allegations stemmed from his criticisms on social media of the draft laws on the Higher Judicial Council and on the Statute for Judges. The Higher Judicial Council's decision is not subject to appeal. A panel suspended another judge, Amal Homani, for six months on similar grounds.

Trial Procedures

The law provides for the right to a fair public trial with the right of appeal, but this did not always occur, especially for those protesting the incorporation of Western Sahara into the country. The law presumes that defendants are innocent. After an initial investigation period in which the order of a prosecutor can detain individuals, defendants are informed promptly of their charges before their trial. Trials are conducted in Arabic, and foreigners have the right to request interpretation if they do not speak Arabic.

Defendants have the right to be present at their trial and to timely consultation with an attorney. In practical terms authorities often denied lawyers timely access to their clients and, in the majority of cases, lawyers met their clients only at the first hearing before the judge. Authorities are required to provide attorneys in cases where the potential sentence is greater than five years, if the defendant is unable to afford one. Publicly provided defense attorneys were often poorly paid and often were neither properly trained in matters pertaining to juveniles nor provided to defendants in a timely fashion. This practice often resulted in inadequate representation. Many NGOs provided attorneys for minors, who frequently did not have the means to pay. Such resources were limited and specific to larger cities. By law defendants in criminal and human rights cases have access to government evidence against them, but judges sometimes prevented or delayed access. The law permits defense attorneys to question witnesses. Despite the provisions of the law, some judges reportedly denied defense requests to question witnesses or to present mitigating witnesses or evidence.

The law forbids judges from admitting confessions made under duress. NGOs reported that the judicial system often relied on confessions for the prosecution of criminal cases, and authorities pressured investigators to obtain a confession from a suspect in order for prosecution to proceed. HRW and local NGOs charged that judges, at their discretion, decided cases based on forced confessions. NGOs alleged this occurred frequently in cases against Sahrawis or individuals accused of terrorism. According to the authorities, police sometimes used claims regarding detainees' statements in place of defendants' confessions when there was a possible question of duress. The country is moving away from a confession-based system to an evidenced-based system. In August the government opened 18 evidence preservation centers throughout the country to preserve the chain of custody of evidence, supporting its change to evidenced-based prosecutions. More than 18,000 police have been trained in recently established evidence collection and preservation procedures to maintain proper chain of custody of evidence in support of evidence-based prosecutions. Police are working with the courts to demonstrate the new evidence preservation rooms to judges to increase their confidence in evidence presented at trials.

Political Prisoners and Detainees

The law does not define or recognize the concept of a political prisoner. The government did not consider any of its prisoners to be political prisoners and stated that it had charged or convicted all individuals in prison under criminal law. Human rights groups, however, refuted this allegation, especially concerning activists advocating Western Sahara's independence.

On July 27, the Court of Cassation granted a new trial before civilian courts for the 22 Gdeim Izik prisoners arrested during the 2010 dismantling of the Gdeim Izik Camp and subsequent violence in Laayoune. Previously convicted in military courts, many NGOs considered the group to be political prisoners. The protesters, 21 of whom remain imprisoned, had been convicted largely on the basis of "confessions" which they alleged had been extracted under torture. Their allegations of torture and other ill-treatment in custody were not investigated. The trial began on December 26; but it was adjourned to January 23, 2017.

Criminal law covers nonviolent advocacy and dissent, such as insulting police in songs or "defaming Morocco's sacred values" by denouncing the king and regime during a public demonstration. Additionally, NGOs, including the Moroccan Association for Human Rights (AMDH), and Sahrawi organizations asserted that the government imprisoned persons for political activities or beliefs under the cover of criminal charges.

Civil Judicial Procedures and Remedies

Although individuals have access to civil courts for lawsuits relating to human rights violations and filed lawsuits, such lawsuits were frequently unsuccessful due to the courts' lack of independence on politically sensitive cases, or lack of impartiality stemming from extrajudicial influence and corruption. There are administrative as well as judicial remedies for alleged wrongs. Authorities sometimes failed to respect court orders.

A National Ombudsman's Office (Mediator Institution) helped to resolve civil matters that did not clear the threshold to merit involvement of the judiciary; it gradually expanded the scope of its activities and subjected complaints to in-depth investigation. Authorities retransmitted to the CNDH for resolution cases specifically related to allegations of human rights abuses against authorities. The CNDH continued to be a conduit through which citizens expressed complaints regarding human rights abuses and violations.

f. Arbitrary or Unlawful Interference with Privacy, Family, Home, or Correspondence

The constitution states an individual's home is inviolable and that a search may take place only with a search warrant; however, authorities at times entered homes without judicial authorization, monitored without legal process personal movement and private communications--including e-mail, text messaging, or other digital communications intended to remain private--and employed informers.

An April 2015 report by Privacy International, based on interviews in 2014 with citizen journalists who covered topics sensitive to the government, recounted incidents of alleged harassment, such as unannounced visits by state officials to the families of the individuals and allegations that their personal computers, websites, and work locations were hacked or tapped.

Section 2. Respect for Civil Liberties, Including:

a. Freedom of Speech and Press

The constitution and law generally provide for freedom of speech and press, although they criminalize and restrict some freedom of expression in the press and social media--specifically criticism of Islam, the institution of the monarchy, and the government's official position regarding territorial integrity and claim to Western Sahara. Such criticism can result in prosecution under the penal code, with punishments ranging from fines to jail time, despite the freedom of expression provided for in the new press code passed in July. There have been no reports of prosecution, however, since the passage of the new press code.

Government-provided figures for the year showed that six journalists or media outlets faced charges for breaches of the national press code, and no journalists are facing charges under the penal code. Seven other journalists or media outlets are facing charges under laws other than the press or penal code. Of the 13 current cases, one was initiated by the government, with the remainder initiated by private citizens, including libel complaints. International and domestic human rights groups criticized criminal prosecutions of journalists and publishers as well as of libel suits, claiming that the government principally used these laws to restrict independent human rights groups and the press and social media.

Freedom of Speech and Expression: The law criminalizes the criticism of Islam, the institution of the monarchy, state institutions, officials such as those in the military, and the government's official position regarding territorial integrity and claim to Western Sahara, and the government actively prosecuted persons who did so.

On January 21, authorities charged journalist and human rights activist, Ali Anouzla, with "undermining national territorial integrity" as a result of comments he made in November 2015 to a German newspaper, which quoted him referring to the "occupied territories" of Western Sahara. Anouzla maintained that he referred to the territory only as "Sahara" and that the paper misquoted him. Several weeks later the paper corrected its translation to use only "Sahara." Subsequently, on May 24, the authorities dropped these charges against Anouzla. At year's end, however, there was no information to confirm charges had been dropped against Anouzla for "supporting," "inciting," and "advocating" terrorism in relation to a 2013 article that linked to a video critical of the king. Trial dates in previous years on these charges were repeatedly postponed.

Press and Media Freedoms: In July parliament passed a new press code that limits punishments for journalistic infractions to fines. The antiterrorism law and the penal code, however, include provisions that permit the government to jail and impose financial penalties on journalists and publishers who violate restrictions related to defamation, libel, and insults. Authorities may impose prison sentences on those convicted of libel. Consequently, self-censorship remained prevalent. Authorities filed charges of libel and other violations of the criminal code against specific journalists, with prosecution of these charges indefinitely delayed.

The government also enforced strict procedures governing NGO representatives and political activists meeting with journalists. Foreign journalists needed, but did not always receive, approval from the Ministry of Communication before meeting with political activists.

In 2015 officials targeted members of the Moroccan Association for Investigative Journalism (AMJI). Authorities detained and questioned several members, including Hicham Mansouri, Maati Monjib, and Hisham Almiraat. On October 26, the trial of the seven AMJI members was postponed to January 2017. At year's end, the individuals remained at liberty but still under investigation although not yet charged.

On June 20, the court of first instance in Casablanca sentenced Hamid El Mahdaoui, editor of a news website, to a four-month suspended prison sentence and 10,000 dirham ($1,000) fine for defamation over a report on the minister of justice's travel expenses.

Violence and Harassment: Authorities subjected some journalists to harassment and intimidation, including attempts to discredit them through harmful rumors about their personal lives. Journalists reported that selective prosecutions served as a mechanism for intimidation.

Censorship or Content Restrictions: Self-censorship and government restrictions on sensitive topics remained serious hurdles to the development of a free, independent, and investigative press. While the government rarely censored the domestic press, it exerted pressure by pursuing legal cases that resulted in heavy fines and suspended publication. Such cases encouraged editors and journalists to self-censor. A Freedom House report this year noted that there is an "atmosphere of fear among journalists" that has led to increased self-censorship. The press code lists threats to public order as one of the criteria for censorship. Publications and broadcast media must also obtain government accreditation. The government may deny and revoke accreditation as well as suspend or confiscate publications. The government claimed that it did not censure, suspend, revoke, or confiscate any registered print, online, television, or radio media outlets from January 2015 to September.

On April 3, a foreign television crew was arrested while filming a report for French station "Canal+" on homosexual activity in the country. Authorities expelled the journalists for working without authorization; the journalists stated that they did not ask for authorization because the subject of their reporting was too sensitive and would not have been approved.

Libel/Slander Laws: Authorities filed charges of libel and other violations of the criminal code against journalists. The new press code includes provisions that permit the government to impose financial penalties on journalists and publishers who violate restrictions related to defamation, libel, and insults. Government statistics indicated 47 cases of defamation, libel, or blasphemy during the year. A court may impose a prison sentence if an individual is unable or unwilling to pay the fine.

National Security: The antiterrorism law provides for the arrest of journalists and filtering websites deemed to "disrupt public order by intimidation, terror, or violence"; however, there were no examples of authorities' use of this provision of the law during the year.

<u>Actions to Expand Press Freedom</u>: In February and July, parliament approved a new press code that provides for freedom of the press and electronic media. The new press code, updated from the 2003 version, replaces prison sentences with fines for violations and provides legal protection for the confidentiality of sources. The press code, however, does not prevent journalists from being charged under the penal code or criminal law if their reporting criticizes Islam, the institution of the monarchy, or the government's official position regarding territorial integrity and claim to Western Sahara.

Internet Freedom

The government did not restrict or disrupt access to the internet, but it did apply laws governing and restricting public speech and the press to the internet. The new press code stipulates that online journalism is equivalent to print journalism. According to Freedom House's current Freedom on the Net report, the government did not block or filter any websites during the year, although laws on combatting terrorism permit filtering websites.

In January the government announced the blockage of voice over internet protocol technology, such as Skype, FaceTime, and Google Voice; however, the government did not block the associated messaging capabilities and the voice services remained available via VPNs. The government indicated that it blocked the services because they did not have proper operating licenses for the country. There was widespread belief among the public and domestic NGOs that blocking these services was not an attempt to limit freedom of speech, but in response to complaints from telecommunications companies that the services were reducing their profits. Shortly following the publication of a Brookings report, citing economic losses of $320 million due to the ban, the government dismissed the head of the National Telecommunications Regulatory Agency, and the ban was lifted in November.

According to a 2015 World Bank estimate, 57 percent of the population used the internet.

Academic Freedom and Cultural Events

By law the government has the right to criminalize presentations or debate questioning the legitimacy of Islam, the monarchy, state institutions, or the status of Western Sahara. The law restricts cultural events and academic activities, although the government generally provided more latitude to political and religious activism confined to university campuses. The Ministry of Interior approved appointments of university rectors.

b. Freedom of Peaceful Assembly and Association

Freedom of Assembly

Legally, groups of more than three persons require authorization from the Ministry of Interior to assemble publicly. Some NGOs complained that authorities did not apply the approval process consistently and have claimed that the government used administrative delays and other methods to suppress or discourage unwanted peaceful assembly. In the absence of authorization, authorities disbanded meetings organized by groups ranging from reformers to student teachers, sometimes with excessive force.

According to HRW's, *World Report 2016*, police allowed many protests demanding political reform and protesting government actions, but on some occasions, they dispersed protestors or prevented demonstrations from occurring.

On January 7, police responded violently to teacher trainees demonstrating peacefully in Inezgane and other cities against new decrees to reduce their stipends and access to employment. According to witnesses police used rubber batons and shields to beat protesters without prior warning to protesters to disperse. Over 150 protesters were injured, including 100 in Inezgane, some with fractures and injuries to the face and head, according to AMDH.

In February, as a result of public outcry against police actions in the January student-teacher protests, the Ministry of Interior launched a training program on nonviolent dispersal of demonstrations and management of peaceful protests in response to complaints about police brutality. Although protests by student teachers continued sporadically into September, police intervention was infrequent after January.

Authorities authorized small public protests on politically sensitive subjects occasionally during the year. For example, in June the Ministry of Interior granted permission for a group of atheist and non-Muslim citizens to protest in front of parliament against an article in the penal code relating to fasting during the Muslim holy month of Ramadan. The protest proceeded and was not dispersed.

A number of civil society contacts reported instances when private event spaces abruptly cancelled bookings, citing official pressure not to allow "controversial" activities on their premises.

Freedom of Association

The constitution and the law provide for freedom of association, although the government sometimes restricted this freedom. The government prohibited or failed to recognize some political opposition groups by deeming them unqualified for NGO status. The government denied official recognition to NGOs that it considered advocates against Islam as the state religion, the monarchy, or territorial integrity.

Authorities obstructed the registration of a number of associations perceived to be critical of the authorities by refusing to accept registration applications or to deliver receipts confirming the lodging of applications.

In June the Spanish NGO International Institute for Non-Violent Action (NOVACT) decided to close its office after the government denied entry to two members of its staff. In May 2015 the government expelled a representative of NOVACT. NOVACT had operated in the country since 2012 (see section 5).

In September 2015 the government requested that HRW suspend its activities in the country. The suspension remained in effect at year's end.

In June 2015 authorities detained and expelled AI research staff. AI engaged in a dialogue with the authorities to resolve obstacles to access; however, some restrictions remained on research as of the end of October.

The Ministry of the Interior required NGOs to register in order to be recognized as a legal entity, but there was no comprehensive national register publicly available. A prospective organization must submit its objectives, bylaws, address, and photocopies of members' identification cards to the ministry. The ministry issues a receipt to the organization that signifies formal approval. If the organization does not receive a receipt within 60 days, it is not formally registered. Unregistered organizations could not access government funds or legally accept contributions.

Several organizations the government chose not to recognize functioned without the receipts, and the government tolerated their activities. The National Federation of Amazigh Associations, an organization supporting the inclusion of the Amazigh population in public life, reported that two Amazigh organizations were denied registration this year. Despite a December 2015 court ruling that the Ministry of Interior had acted inappropriately in refusing to receive a petition by the Moroccan AMDH to renew their permit to operate a local branch in Temara, the organization continued to report difficulties in renewing registrations in multiple locations in the country even after court decisions in their favor.

On November 7, authorities informed historian Maati Monjib that the administrative court in Rabat ruled that the Ministry of Interior had acted inappropriately in refusing to register his NGO Freedom Now. The court ordered the ministry to pay a fine and grant Freedom Now's registration request.

Authorities continued to monitor Justice and Charity Organization activities.

c. Freedom of Religion

See the Department of State's *International Religious Freedom Report* at www.state.gov/religiousfreedomreport/.

d. Freedom of Movement, Internally Displaced Persons, Protection of Refugees, and Stateless Persons

The law provides for freedom of internal movement, foreign travel, emigration, and repatriation, and the government generally respected these rights.

Abuse of Migrants, Refugees, and Stateless Persons: Refugees and asylum seekers, as well as migrants, were particularly vulnerable to abuse; however, in contrast to previous years, following the 2014 migrant regularization program, there were fewer reports of mass arrests and brutalization by security forces of sub-Saharan migrants and of abuse by criminal gangs involved in human trafficking. There were reports of government authorities arresting or detaining migrants, particularly around the Spanish enclave cities of Melilla and Ceuta, and forcibly relocating them to other cities in the country (see section 1.d.).

In-country Movement: The law provides for freedom of internal movement. Authorities generally respected this right.

Exile: While the law provides for forced exile, there were no instances of forced exile during the year.

<u>Emigration and Repatriation</u>: The government encouraged the return of Sahrawi refugees from Algeria and elsewhere if they acknowledged the government's authority over Western Sahara. The government continued to make travel documents available to Sahrawis, and there were no reported cases of authorities preventing Sahrawis from traveling out of the country. On August 22, media reported that authorities prevented Salem Bachir, also known as Salem Hamda or M'Hamed Salem Hamda Birouk, the POLISARIO "Ambassador" to Argentina, from entering the territory at the airport in Laayoune. According to authorities, they prevented Bachir's entry in the interest of public security.

Protection of Refugees

The government cooperated with the Office of the UN High Commissioner for Refugees (UNHCR) and other humanitarian organizations in providing protection and assistance to refugees, returning refugees, asylum seekers, and other persons of concern. The government also provided funding to humanitarian organizations to provide social services to migrants, including refugees. As of October 31, UNHCR registered 1,151 Syrians. UNHCR referred cases meeting the criteria for refugee recognition to the government's interministerial Commission in Charge of Hearings for Asylum Seekers within the Bureau of Refugees and Stateless Persons, and 70 non-Syrian individuals were granted status as of the end of November. The government continued to grant status to UNHCR-recognized refugees and temporary status to registered Syrians. According to UNHCR statistics, since 2013 the Commission in Charge of Hearings for Asylum Seekers has recognized as refugees 696 non-Syrians referred by UNHCR.

<u>Access to Asylum</u>: The law provides for the granting of refugee status. The government has historically deferred to UNHCR as the sole agency in the country entitled to perform refugee status determinations and verify asylum cases. The government recognizes two types of asylum status: refugees designated according to the UNHCR statute and the "exceptional regularization of persons in irregular situation." In 2015 the government continued to provide "exceptional regularization" to Syrians seeking international protection.

On December 15, the government launched the second phase of its migrant regularization program to provide legal status to migrants in exceptional circumstances. This program, similar to the 2014 campaign, will grant legal status to foreign spouses and children of citizens and other legal residents of the country, as well as individuals with at least five years of residence in the country, a valid work contract, or chronic illness.

<u>Access to Basic Services</u>: Recognized refugees were able to gain access to health care and education services. Asylum seekers were, however, often unable to access the national health care system and continued to have little access to the judicial system until recognized as refugees. Registered refugees and regularized migrants have the right to work.

Section 3. Freedom to Participate in the Political Process

The law provides for, and citizens participated in, regular, free elections based on universal suffrage and conducted by secret ballot providing for the free expression of the will of the people for parliament's Chamber of Representatives and municipal and regional councils. Regional and professional bodies indirectly elected members of parliament's less powerful Chamber of Counselors.

The king may dissolve parliament in consultation with the head of government (prime minister) and can rule by decree. The king presides over the Council of Ministers, the supreme decision-making body, except in cases when he delegates that authority to the head of government. The king presides over the Supreme Security Council and the Ulema Council (Council of Senior Religious Scholars).

As head of state, the king appoints the head of government. The constitution obliges the king to choose the head of government from the party with the most elected seats in the Chamber of Representatives. The constitution authorizes the head of government to nominate all government ministers, although the king must approve these nominations. Royal advisors work in coordinating roles with respective government ministries.

A national referendum, the results of which require the king's approval, or a bill submitted by the king that receives two-thirds majority approval from both legislative chambers can amend the constitution.

Elections and Political Participation

<u>Recent Elections</u>: On October 7, the country held direct elections for the Chamber of Representatives (lower house of parliament), during which the Party of Justice and Development (PJD) won the most seats. As stipulated by the constitution, the King tasked PJD, as the party with the most seats in the newly elected chamber, to form a governing coalition and nominate new ministers.

The CNDH was the leading institution monitoring the election. The Electoral Accreditation Commission, presided over by the CNDH with the participation of the Interministerial Delegation for Human Rights (DIDH), the Central Authority for the Prevention of Corruption (ICPC), and 32 domestic associations accredited 4,365 domestic observers. An additional 316 international observers took part in election monitoring. The major political parties and the vast majority of the domestic observers considered the elections free, fair, and transparent. Most international observers considered them credible elections in which voters were able to choose freely and deemed the process free of systemic irregularities.

Political Parties and Political Participation: Political parties faced fewer government-imposed restrictions under the 2011 Constitution. The Ministry of Interior applied laws that made it easier for political parties to register. A political party may not legally challenge Islam as the state religion, the institution of the monarchy, or the country's territorial integrity. The law prohibits basing a party on a religious, ethnic, or regional identity.

Participation of Women and Minorities: Female politicians featured prominently in media on a variety of matters, but authorities largely excluded them from senior decision-making positions. The elections increased participation of women in the Chamber of Representatives from 17 percent to 21 percent. Voters elected a record number of women in the October 7 elections, although very few subsequently won leadership positions as ministers or parliamentary committee presidents.

Section 4. Corruption and Lack of Transparency in Government

The law provides criminal penalties for corruption by officials, but the government generally did not implement the law effectively. Officials often engaged in corrupt practices with impunity. Corruption was a serious problem in the executive branch, including police, as well as in the legislative and judicial branches.

Corruption: There were reports of mostly petty government corruption, but authorities investigated few cases and successfully prosecuted at least nine during the last two years. There was a widespread perception of serious government corruption, but there were few reports of mid- or high-level corruption. Generally, observers considered corruption a serious problem, with insufficient governmental checks and balances to reduce its occurrence. According to government statistics, the Gendarmerie Royale questioned 41,848 public officials in 2015 for corruption offenses. As of October 12, an additional 16,572 officials had been questioned. Information on the results of the interrogations was not available.

The king, who has made statements calling for judicial system reform since 2009, acknowledged the judiciary's lack of independence and susceptibility to influence. Many members of the well-entrenched and conservative judicial community were loath to adopt new procedures. In some cases judges received disciplinary sanctions for corruption, but were not prosecuted.

Observers noted widespread corruption among police. The government claimed to investigate corruption and other instances of police malfeasance through an internal mechanism (see section 1.d.).

The ICPC is responsible for combating corruption. In May 2015 parliament adopted a constitutionally mandated law providing the ICPC with the authority to compel government institutions to comply with anticorruption investigations. According to government figures, the ICPC received 398 formal complaints or denunciations through October (compared to 400 in all of 2014). The ICPC forwarded to the general prosecutor 55 cases of corruption during the year. Legal penalties for corruption were rare, with the government reporting that as of October, 334 public officials were prosecuted for corruption. Conviction and sentencing information was unavailable.

In addition to the ICPC, the Ministry of Justice and the High Audit Institution (government accountability court) had jurisdiction over corruption issues, but they did not pursue any high-profile cases during the year. The Ministry of Justice ran a hotline for the public to report instances of corruption. According to Ministry of Justice statistics, the hotline received an average of 2,000 calls per day during the first half of the year. As a result of calls, 12 cases were opened, resulting in nine sentences of prison time and fines, two closed for lack of evidence, and one that remains under investigation.

Financial Disclosure: The law requires judges, ministers, and members of parliament to submit financial disclosure statements to the High Audit Institution, which is responsible for monitoring and verifying disclosure compliance. According to allegations from government transparency groups, however, many officials did not file disclosures. There are no effective criminal or administrative sanctions for noncompliance.

<u>Public Access to Information</u>: There is no freedom of information law, although a draft law on public access to information law was passed by the lower house of parliament on July 20. At year's end, the law is pending a vote in the upper house, before it can be sent to the Council of Ministers and king for approval. The constitution provides for citizen access to information held by public institutions, but authorities did not provide a dedicated access mechanism. The government rarely granted access to official information to citizens and noncitizens, including foreign media. Public officials received no training on access to information. There were no public outreach activities regarding public access to information.

Section 5. Governmental Attitude Regarding International and Nongovernmental Investigation of Alleged Violations of Human Rights

Groups investigated and published findings on human rights cases; however, the government's responsiveness to, cooperation with, and restrictions on domestic and international human rights organizations varied, depending on its evaluation of the political orientation of the organization and the sensitivity of the issues.

On January 26, according to reports, authorities expelled Andrea Nusse, the country director for Friedrich Naumann Foundation, a German NGO promoting human rights, rule of law, and democracy. Nusse had been country director for the foundation for the past three years. According to the organization, this action was taken because the organization awarded an international human rights award to government critic, Ali Anouzla. Authorities asserted that Nusse's residency expired in August 2015, she left the country of her own accord in December 2015, and returned briefly in January to take care of her personal affairs. She was never the subject of an expulsion order.

On June 29, the International Institute for Nonviolent Action (NOVACT), a Spain-based NGO, decided to close its office citing government pressure since June 2015, including refusal to register the organization and expulsion or refusal of entry for its staff members. The organization claims that its difficulties were related to its support for rights for the LGBTI community. The government stated that the registration and entry refusals were due to improperly filed paperwork.

Following disputes between AI and governmental authorities in 2015, AI held a series of exchanges with the government during the year, but the issue of permitting international researchers to travel to the country remained unresolved by September. In late September, AI was prevented from holding its annual youth camp as scheduled. The Ministry of Interior claimed that it requested the postponement of the camp due to the electoral period. At the end of the year, AI had still not held the annual camp.

The government ordered HRW to suspend activities in 2015. In March, HRW met with the government but was informed that the suspension remained in place until further notice. Through September, HRW has been unable to conduct activities in the country. Nevertheless, HRW researchers have been able to engage with the government electronically and continue to publish limited information on the situation in the country.

The government recognized several domestic human rights NGOs with national coverage. The Moroccan Organization for Human Rights and the AMDH were the largest domestic human rights organizations.

During the year activists and NGOs reported continuing restrictions on their activities in the country. According to the AMDH, authorities prohibited 111 of its scheduled activities between June 2014 and June. Many activists reported that rather than banning activities outright, the government allegedly resorted to restricting the use of public spaces and conference rooms, as well as informing the proprietors of private spaces that certain activities should not be welcome. Organizations claimed that government officials told them their events were cancelled for failing to follow required procedures for public meetings, although the organizations say they submitted the necessary paperwork except in cases where they believed the law does not require it. Some unrecognized NGOs that did not cooperate officially with the government still shared information informally with both the government and government-affiliated organizations.

During the year the government occasionally met with and responded to inquiries and recommendations from NGOs.

<u>Government Human Rights Bodies</u>: There are three governmental human rights entities.

The CNDH is a national human rights institution established by the constitution that operates independently from the elected government. It is publicly funded and operates in conformity with the Principles of Paris according to the Global Alliance of National Human Rights Institutions, which recognized it in November 2015 as a "class A national human rights institution" within the UN framework. It served as the principal advisory body to the king and government on human rights. The council filled the role of a national human rights monitoring mechanism for preventing torture, in keeping with the government's international obligations. Additionally, the CNDH produced reports during the year criticizing current and former government practices in the domains of freedom of expression and assembly as well as women's rights and published guides on political rights for youth activists and journalists. In 2014 the CNDH established the National Human Rights Training Institute (INFDH), which partners with international organizations to provide training to civil society, media, law enforcement, medical personnel, educators, and legal practitioners. Between January and November, the INFDH provided 39 training sessions on election observation, discrimination, human rights in the workplace, and the investigation and prevention of torture.

The Mediator Institution acted as a more general ombudsman. It considered allegations of governmental injustices and had the power to carry out inquiries and investigations, propose disciplinary action, or refer cases to the public prosecutor.

The mission of the DIDH is to promote the protection of human rights across all ministries, serve as a government interlocutor with domestic and international NGOs, and interact with relevant UN bodies regarding international human rights obligations. The DIDH has the primary responsibility for coordinating government responses to UN bodies on adherence to treaty obligations.

Section 6. Discrimination, Societal Abuses, and Trafficking in Persons

Women

Rape and Domestic Violence: The law punishes men convicted of rape with prison terms of five to 10 years; when the conviction involves a minor, the prison sentence ranges from 10 to 20 years. Spousal rape is not a crime. A sexual assault conviction may result in a prison sentence of up to one year and a fine of 15,000 dirhams ($1,530). Police were slow to act in domestic violence cases, and the government generally did not enforce the law and sometimes returned women against their will to abusive homes. Victims did not report the vast majority of sexual assaults to police due to social pressure, which would most likely hold the victim responsible. Police selectively investigated cases; among the minority brought to trial, successful prosecutions were rare. In 2013 articles of the penal code that criminalized hiding or subverting the search for a married woman, which in effect made domestic violence shelters illegal, were repealed.

Domestic violence was widespread. Statistics on rape or sexual assault were unreliable due to underreporting; no survey on the subject has been conducted since 2009. A Bureau of Statistics 2013 planning publication, *The Moroccan Woman, by the Numbers*, revealed that 63 percent of women reported suffering an act of violence in the preceding year, although the study based these figures on the 2009 survey. Various domestic advocacy groups, such as the Democratic League for Women's Rights, estimated that husbands perpetrated eight of 10 cases of violence against women.

Prior to 2014 rapists could avoid punishment by marrying the victim. A 2014 amendment to the penal code disallows rapists' exoneration through marriage to their victims. Nonetheless, numerous articles of the penal code pertaining to rape perpetuate unequal treatment for women and provide insufficient protection, despite 2009 revisions to the family law.

The law does not specifically prohibit domestic violence against women, but the general prohibitions of the criminal code address such violence. Legally, high-level misdemeanors occur when a victim's injuries result in 20 days of disability leave from work. Low-level misdemeanors occur when a victim's disability lasts for less than 20 days. According to NGOs the courts rarely prosecuted perpetrators of low-level misdemeanors. Police generally treated domestic violence as a social rather than a criminal matter. Statistics provided by the government indicated that it provided direct support to 45 counseling centers for female victims of violence, and indirect support to 97 others, as part of a broader effort to support projects benefitting women in society.

Physical abuse was legal grounds for divorce, although few women reported such abuse to authorities. Domestic violence mediation generally occurred within the family. Women choosing legal action generally preferred pursuing divorce in family courts rather than criminal prosecutions.

A small number of groups, such as the Anaruz Network and the Democratic League for Women's Rights, were available to provide assistance and guidance to victims. Counseling centers existed exclusively in urban areas. Services for victims of violence in rural areas were generally limited to those provided by local police.

The government funded a number of women's shelters under the Ministry of Solidarity, Women, Family, and Social Development. A few NGOs made efforts to provide shelter for victims of domestic abuse. There were reports, however, that these shelters were not accessible to persons with disabilities. Courts had "victims of abuse cells" that brought together prosecutors, lawyers, judges, women's NGO representatives, and hospital personnel to review domestic and child abuse cases to provide for the best interests of women or children according to proper procedure.

Many domestic NGOs worked to advance women's rights and promote women's issues. Among these were the Democratic Association of Moroccan Women, the Union for Women's Action, the Democratic League for Women's Rights, Mobilizing for Rights Associates, and the Moroccan Association for Women's Rights. All advocated enhanced political and civil rights for women. NGOs also promoted literacy and taught women basic hygiene, family planning, and childcare.

Sexual Harassment: Sexual harassment in the workplace is criminal only when it is an abuse of authority by a superior, as stipulated by the penal code. Violations are punishable by one to two years' imprisonment and a fine of 5,000 to 50,000 dirhams ($511 to $5,108). Authorities did not effectively enforce laws against sexual harassment. According to the government, although the law allows victims to sue employers, only a few did so. The government reported that 36 cases of sexual harassment were filed during 2015. Most women feared losing their job as a result or worried about proving the charge. NGOs reported widespread sexual harassment contributed to the low rate of female participation in the labor force, although the total number of violent acts reported was extremely low and likely not representative of the real number of incidents in the country.

Reproductive Rights: Individuals and couples have the right to decide the number, spacing, and timing of their children; manage their reproductive health; and have access to the information and means to do so, free from discrimination, coercion, or violence. Authorities generally did not discriminate against women in accessing sexual and reproductive health care, including for sexually transmitted infections. Contraception is legal, and most forms were widely available. According to the Population Reference Bureau, the country has invested in increasing the availability of voluntary family planning services, expanding and improving maternal health care, and providing for access to obstetric care by eliminating fees.

The contraceptive pill is available over the counter, without a prescription. Skilled health attendance at delivery and postpartum care were available for women who could afford it, with approximately 74 percent of overall births attended by skilled health personnel. In June the government proposed a draft law authorizing abortion in cases of rape, incest, or severe deformation, expanding existing legislation that allowed abortion in case of danger to the life of the mother.

The most recent UN statistics showed there were approximately 121 maternal deaths per 100,000 live births in the country in 2015 and that 57 percent of women between the ages of 15 and 49 years old used a modern method of contraception in 2011. The major factors influencing maternal mortality and contraceptive prevalence rates were female illiteracy, lack of knowledge about availability of services, cost of services, social pressure against contraceptive use, and limited availability of transportation to health centers and hospitals for those in rural areas.

<u>Discrimination</u>: The constitution provides women equal rights in civil, political, economic, cultural, and environmental affairs. The law requires equal pay for equal work, although in practice this did not occur. Numerous problems related to discrimination against women remained, both with enforcement of equal rights provided for by the laws and constitution and in the reduced rights provided to women in inheritance. Implementation of laws and reforms met considerable resistance from men in certain areas of the country. Despite lobbying by women's NGOs, enforcement of these property laws remained inconsistent.

According to the law, women are entitled to a share of inherited property, but a woman's share of inheritance is less than that of a man. Generally, women are entitled to receive half the inheritance a man would receive in the same circumstances. A sole male heir would receive the entire estate, while a sole female heir would receive half the estate with the rest going to other relatives. The 2004 reform of the family code did not change inheritance laws, which the constitution does not specifically address.

The family code places the family under the joint responsibility of both spouses, makes divorce available by mutual consent, and places legal limits on polygamy. Implementation of family law reforms remained a problem. The judiciary lacked willingness to enforce them, as many judges did not agree with their provisions. Corruption among working-level court clerks and lack of knowledge about its provisions among lawyers were also obstacles to enforcement of the law. Widespread female illiteracy also limited women's ability to navigate the legal system.

There were few legal obstacles to women's participation in business and other economic activities. According to some entrepreneurs and NGOs, however, women had difficulty accessing credit and owning and managing businesses. Rural women faced restrictions on education and employment opportunities for social and cultural reasons. Trade unions did not have women represented in leadership positions.

The government led some efforts to improve the status of women in the workplace, most notably the constitutional mandate for the creation of an Authority for Gender Parity and Fighting All Forms of Discrimination, an institution that was being developed jointly between parliament and the CNDH, but remained unimplemented at year's end. In October 2015 the CNDH issued a report citing continued widespread gender inequality and advocating reforms in line with the constitution, including creation of an independent and empowered Authority for Gender Parity and Fighting All Forms of Discrimination; changes to the family code; and reforms to the system of inheritance away from religious-based rules to one that ensures equality of men and women. Women's rights NGOs continued to press the government to codify women's rights in formal legislation.

Children

Birth Registration: The law permits both parents to pass nationality to their children. There were, nonetheless, cases in which authorities denied identification papers to children because they were born to unmarried parents. In cases of undocumented children, NGOs, magistrates, and attorneys advocated for the children. The process of obtaining necessary identification papers was lengthy and arduous if not completed within 30 days of a child's birth. According to press reports and Amazigh NGOs, during the year representatives of the Ministry of Interior refused to register the births of some children whose parents sought to give them Amazigh names.

Education: Education is free and compulsory through age 15 years old. Girls' representation in education in recent years improved significantly, especially in urban areas.

Child Abuse: NGOs, human rights groups, media outlets, and the UN Children's Fund claimed child abuse was widespread, although the government noted that reports are decreasing. Government statistics showed 6,830 cases of child abuse investigated this year, and 7,526 cases investigated in 2015. Anecdotal evidence showed that abuse of child domestic servants was a problem. On July 26, parliament passed a law prohibiting children under the age of 16 years old from working as domestic servants and strictly limiting the work of children under the age of 18 (see section 7.c.). Prosecutions for child abuse were extremely rare.

The Ministry of Youth and Sports managed 18 child protection centers, with five reserved specifically for girls. The centers house delinquents, homeless children, victims of domestic violence, drug addicts, and other "children in distress" who have not committed a crime, as well as children who have committed crimes or minor infractions but whom a court determines should not be housed in a juvenile "reform and education center" run by the prison administration. This mingling of children in conflict with the law and children in distress also occurred during other stages of the process. The centers provided educational and professional training, with a goal of reintegrating the minors into the society. While the budgets of the centers were low, conditions varied because some centers received charitable gifts.

Early and Forced Marriage: The legal age for marriage is 18 years old, but parents, with the informed consent of the minor, may secure a waiver from a judge for underage marriage. The judiciary approved the vast majority of petitions for underage marriages. Child marriage remained a concern.

Sexual Exploitation of Children: The age of consent is 18 years old. Penalties for sexual exploitation of children range from two years' to life imprisonment and fines from 9,550 dirhams ($960) to 344,000 dirhams ($34,600). Convicted rapists and pedophiles are not eligible for pardons. Children engaged in prostitution, and the country was a destination for sex tourism. The penal code also provides punishment for child pornography.

During the year the government reported undertaking actions to implement its child protection policy adopted in 2014 and overseen by the Ministry of Solidarity, Women, Family, and Social Development. Actions included cooperating with internet providers to protect children from exploitation and provide safe internet access; developing a responsible tourism communication strategy, in cooperation with the Ministry of Tourism, to protect children; and raising awareness in the private tourism sector of children's rights and preventing child sex tourism in accordance with the World Trade Organization's global code of ethics.

Also see the Department of Labor's *Findings on the Worst Forms of Child Labor* at www.dol.gov/ilab/reports/child-labor/findings.

International Child Abductions: The country is a party to the 1980 Hague Convention on the Civil Aspects of International Child Abduction. See the Department of State's *Annual Report on International Parental Child Abduction* at https://travel.state.gov/content/childabduction/en/legal/compliance.html.

Anti-Semitism

Community leaders estimated the size of the Jewish population at 4,000. Overall, there appeared to be little overt anti-Semitism. The government protects and supports the Jewish community. The government provided appropriate security and Jews generally lived in safety. The community noted that tensions escalated when there was rising hostility between Israel and the Palestinians, although reports of anti-Semitic acts were rare.

Trafficking in Persons

See the Department of State's *Trafficking in Persons Report* at www.state.gov/j/tip/rls/tiprpt/.

Persons with Disabilities

The law prohibits discrimination against persons with physical, sensory, intellectual, and mental disabilities in employment, education, and access to health care. The law also provides for regulations and building codes that provide for access for persons with disabilities. The government did not effectively enforce or implement these laws and regulations. While building codes enacted in 2003 require accessibility for all persons, the codes exempt most pre-2003 structures, and authorities rarely enforced them for new construction. Most public transportation was inaccessible to persons with disabilities, although the national rail system offered wheelchair ramps, handicap-accessible bathrooms, and special seating areas. Government policy provides that persons with disabilities should have equal access to information and communications. Special communication devices for persons with visual or audio disabilities were not widely available.

The Ministry of Social Development, Family, and Solidarity has responsibility for protecting the rights of persons with disabilities and attempted to integrate persons with disabilities into society by implementing a quota of 7 percent for persons with disabilities in vocational training in the public sector and 5 percent in the private sector. Both sectors were far from achieving the quotas. The government maintained more than 400 integrated classes for children with learning disabilities, but private charities and civil society organizations were primarily responsible for integration. Families typically supported persons with disabilities, although some survived by begging.

National/Racial/Ethnic Minorities

Many of the poorest regions in the country, particularly the Middle Atlas region, were predominantly Amazigh and had illiteracy rates higher than the national average. Basic governmental services in this mountainous and underdeveloped region were not extensive. Official languages are Arabic and Amazigh, although Arabic predominates. Instruction in the Amazigh language is mandatory for students at the interior ministry's School for Administrators in Kenitra. French and Amazigh materials were available in the news media and, to a much lesser extent, educational institutions. On September 26, the Council of Ministers approved and sent to parliament for debate a draft law to implement the constitutional provision making Amazigh an official language. Parliament, however, was out of session and had not debated the law by year's end.

The majority of the population, including the royal family, claimed some Amazigh heritage. Amazigh cultural groups contended they were rapidly losing their traditions and language to Arabization. The government provided television programs in the three national Amazigh dialects of Tarifit, Tashelhit, and Tamazight. The government has previously reported that it offered Amazigh language classes in the curriculum of 30 percent of schools. A lack of qualified teachers hindered otherwise expanding Amazigh language education. The palace-funded Royal Institute of Amazigh Culture created a university-level teacher-training program to eliminate the shortage of qualified teachers.

For more information regarding the situation of Sahrawis in Moroccan-administered Western Sahara, see the Department of State's 2016 annual *Country Reports on Human Rights* for Western Sahara.

Acts of Violence, Discrimination, and Other Abuses Based on Sexual Orientation and Gender Identity

The penal code criminalizes consensual same-sex sexual activity with a maximum sentence of three years in prison. Same-sex marriage is not legally possible. Media and the public addressed questions of sexuality, sexual orientation, and gender identity more openly than in previous years.

The law criminalizes homosexual acts or "acts against nature," as well as all sexual activity outside of marriage regardless of sexual orientation. Antidiscrimination laws do not apply to LGBTI persons, and the penal code does not criminalize hate crimes. There was a stigma against LGBTI persons, but there were no reports of discrimination based on sexual orientation or gender identity in employment, housing, access to education, or health care. Authorities prosecuted individuals engaged in same-sex sexual activity at least once during the year.

In one widely publicized case, on October 27, authorities arrested two minors, 16 and 17 years old, in Marrakech for "homosexuality" after one of the girls' relatives saw them kissing and reported them to police. Media and NGOs reported that after a week in pretrial detention, the girls were granted provisional release pending a trial. On December 9, the two were found innocent.

Sexual orientation and gender identity constituted a basis for societal violence, harassment, blackmail, or other actions, generally at a local level, although with reduced frequency. There were reports of societal discrimination, physical violence, or harassment based on sexual orientation or gender identity.

For example, in March observers filmed a mob in Beni Mellal attacking two men presumed to be gay. The mob attacked the men in their home before making them undress and walk through the city's streets to a police station, where the two were arrested and charged with homosexuality. Authorities later arrested several of the men involved in the attack. The court sentenced the attackers to between three and six months and gave suspended sentences to the two individuals accused of homosexual acts.

HIV and AIDS Social Stigma

Persons with HIV/AIDS faced discrimination and had limited treatment options. A recent Afrobarometer poll reported that 60 percent of Moroccans would not welcome an HIV positive individual as their neighbor. The Joint UN Program on HIV/AIDS reported that some health-care providers were reluctant to treat persons with HIV/AIDS due to fear of infection. There are currently 16 HIV/AIDS treatment centers countrywide. There were domestic NGOs focused on treating HIV/AIDS patients.

Section 7. Worker Rights

a. Freedom of Association and the Right to Collective Bargaining

The constitution provides workers with the rights to form and join unions, strike, and bargain collectively, with some restrictions. The current law prohibits certain categories of government employees, including members of the armed forces, police, and some members of the judiciary from forming and joining unions and from conducting strikes. The law excludes migrant workers from assuming leadership positions in unions.

According to the labor code, employer and worker representatives should conduct discussions to agree on the wages and employment conditions of unionized workers. The law allows several independent unions to exist but requires 35 percent of the total employee base to be associated with a union for the union to be representative and engage in collective bargaining. The law prohibits antiunion discrimination and prohibits companies from dismissing workers for participating in legitimate union-organizing activities. Courts have the authority to reinstate workers dismissed arbitrarily and may enforce rulings that compel employers to pay damages and back pay.

The law concerning strikes requires compulsory arbitration of disputes, prohibits sit-ins, and calls for a 10-day notice of a strike. The government may intervene in strikes. A strike may not take place over matters covered in a collective contract for one year after the contract comes into force. The government has the authority to disperse strikers in public areas not authorized for demonstrations and to prevent the unauthorized occupancy of private space. Unions may neither engage in sabotage nor prevent those individuals who were not on strike from working.

The government did not adequately enforce labor laws due to a lack of inspection personnel and resources. Inspectors do not have punitive power and cannot levy fines or other punishments. Upon action of the state prosecutor, the courts can force the employer to take remedial actions through a court decree. Penalties were not sufficient to deter violations. Regulations also required inspectors to serve as mediators in disputes, requiring them to spend a significant amount of time in their offices, not conducting inspections. Enforcement procedures were subjected to lengthy delays and appeals.

The government generally respected freedom of association and the right to collective bargaining. Employers limited the scope of collective bargaining, frequently setting wages unilaterally for the majority of unionized and nonunionized workers. Domestic NGOs reported that employers often used temporary contracts to discourage employees from affiliating with or organizing unions. Legally, unions can negotiate with the government on national-level labor issues. From April 12 to May 4, the government held its first formal traditional tripartite social dialogue session since 2012, largely to discuss a pending pension reform legislation that was later passed in parliament despite union protests. At the sectoral level, trade unions negotiated with private employers concerning minimum wage, compensation, and other concerns.

Labor disputes were common and, in some cases, the result of employers failing to implement collective bargaining agreements and withholding wages. Trade unions complained that the government at times used the penal code to prosecute workers for striking and to suppress strikes. Most union federations strongly allied with political parties, but unions were generally free from government interference.

b. Prohibition of Forced or Compulsory Labor

The law prohibits all forms of forced or compulsory labor. The law penalizes forced adult labor by a fine for the first offense and a jail term of up to three months for subsequent offenses. Penalties for forced child labor under the law range from one to three years' imprisonment. Authorities did not adequately enforce the legislation. Reports indicated that forced labor, especially of children, occurred (see section 7.c.).

On August 22, the government approved a law regulating the employment of domestic workers, who had previously been exempted from labor law. The new law includes provisions on the employment of minors as domestic servants (see section 7.c.). Penalties for violating this law start with a fine and, in cases of repeated offense, can include one to three months' imprisonment.

Labor inspectors did not inspect small workshops and private homes where the majority of such practices occurred, as the law requires a warrant to search a private residence. The small number of inspectors, the scarce resources at their disposal, and the broad geographic dispersion of sites also limited effective enforcement of the law.

Local NGOs reported that an undetermined number of Filipina and Indonesian domestic workers filed suits against their former employers. These suits included significant indicators of potential trafficking abuses, such as withholding passports or wages. Information on disposition of these cases was not available. Also see the Department of State's *Trafficking in Persons Report* at www.state.gov/j/tip/rls/tiprpt/.

c. Prohibition of Child Labor and Minimum Age for Employment

The minimum age for employment in most sectors is 15 years old. The law prohibits children younger than 16 years old from working in domestic work, and younger than 18 years old from working in 33 "hazardous" sectors (see section 7.e.). In all sectors children younger than 16 years old are prohibited from working more than 10 hours per day; employers must give them a break of at least one hour. The law does not permit children younger than 16 years old to work between the hours of 9 p.m. and 6 a.m. in nonagricultural work or between 8 p.m. and 5 a.m. in agriculture. The overwhelming majority of child laborers worked in rural areas, according to the government's statistical agency, the High Planning Commission. The law excludes seasonal agricultural work and work in traditional artisanal or handicraft sectors of businesses with fewer than five employees. The law prohibits employment of children younger than 18 years old in stone quarries, mines, fishing, or any other positions the government considers hazardous. Some families from rural areas sent girls to work as domestics in urban areas. Boys experienced forced labor as apprentices in the artisan and construction industries and in mechanic shops.

The Ministry of Employment and Social Affairs is responsible for implementing and enforcing child labor laws and regulations. The law provides for legal sanctions against employers who recruit children under 15 years old, with fines ranging from 27,000 to 32,000 dirhams ($2,710 to $3,210). Punishment for violations of the child labor laws includes criminal penalties, civil fines, and withdrawal or suspension of one or more civil, national, or family rights, including denial of legal residence in the country for five to 10 years. Penalties were not sufficient to deter violations.

The ministry did not systematically inspect workplaces or enforce sanctions against child labor. During the year the 51 national labor inspectorates had 53 inspectors trained in child labor issues and designated as a "focal point." According to various reports, police, prosecutors, and judges rarely enforced legal provisions on "forced labor in cases involving child domestics," and few parents of children working as domestics were willing or able to pursue legal avenues likely to provide any direct benefit.

Authorities successfully prosecuted employers throughout the year for employing a child domestic worker, but labor inspectors responsible for enforcing the labor code do not have jurisdiction to inspect private residences, as inspection requires a warrant. Stakeholders reported limited government coordination on providing services to reintegrate children removed from child labor with many agencies performing overlapping roles with unclear responsibilities that led to gaps in child reintegration.

The government expanded coordination with local, national, and international NGOs on education and training programs to combat child labor during the year. The Ministry of Employment and Social Affairs, led by the Office of the Director of Work in conjunction with NGOs, oversaw programs dealing with child labor. The programs sought to decrease the incidence of child labor by raising awareness of the problem, providing financial assistance to needy families, and lowering obstacles for at-risk children to attend school. Additionally, public education was available to migrant children, lowering their vulnerability to child labor.

The Ministry of Employment and Social Affairs reported that in 2015 (the most recent annualized inspection information available) inspectors conducted 443 visits to different private sector enterprises. During these visits they made 2,214 official "observations." Authorities removed 63 children younger than 15 years old from work and also removed 265 children between the ages of 15 and 18 years old from hazardous work. There was no detailed information available on the collection of fines or on assistance to children identified through inspections.

Observers reported noncompliance with child labor laws in agriculture and private urban residences.

Some children became apprentices before they were 12 years old, particularly in small family-run workshops in the handicraft industry. Children also worked in hazardous occupations as designated by law. These included fishing and, in the informal sector, in textiles, light manufacturing, and carpet weaving. Children's safety, health conditions, and wages were often substandard.

In some cases employers subjected children to the worst forms of child labor, including commercial sexual exploitation, sometimes as the result of human trafficking (see section 6, Children); forced domestic work, sometimes as the result of human trafficking; and forced labor in the production of artisan crafts and construction.

NGOs documented the physical and psychological abuse of children employed as domestic servants. Employers paid parents for their children's work. Most child domestics received food, lodging, and clothing instead of monetary compensation, or employers paid them significantly below the minimum wage.

The High Planning Commission reported continued reduction in child labor, claiming that by the end of 2015 approximately 59,000 children between the ages of seven and 15 years old worked, compared with 68,870 in 2014 and 88, 570 in 2013.

Also see the Department of Labor's *Findings on the Worst Forms of Child Labor* at www.dol.gov/ilab/reports/child-labor/findings.

d. Discrimination with Respect to Employment and Occupation

The labor code prohibits discrimination with respect to employment and occupation on the basis of race, color, gender, disability, marital status, religion, political opinion, trade union affiliation, national ancestry, or social origin, resulting in a violation or alteration of the principle of equal opportunity or treatment on equal footing regarding employment or the practice of a profession. This was true in particular with regard to recruitment, conduct and labor distribution, vocational training, wages, advances, the granting of social benefits, disciplinary measures, and dismissal. The law does not address sexual orientation, gender identity, age, language, HIV-positive status, or other communicable diseases in this context. The law provides for equal pay for equal work. The law prohibits the employment of women and youths (between the ages of 15 and 17 years old) in certain occupations that authorities considered hazardous, such as mining.

Discrimination in all categories prohibited by law occurred, as the government lacked sufficient human and financial resources to enforce these laws effectively. Migrant worker organizations reported that some migrants experienced discrimination in hiring, wages, or conditions of employment.

e. Acceptable Conditions of Work

The minimum wage was 108 dirhams ($11.13) per day in the industrialized sector, 70 dirhams ($7.22) per day for agricultural workers, and 65 dirhams ($6.70) per day for domestic workers. The World Bank established the absolute poverty level threshold wage as 70 dirhams ($7.22) per day. Including traditional holiday-related bonuses, workers generally received the equivalent of 13 to 16 months' salary each year. Informal businesses employed approximately 60 percent of the labor force and often ignored minimum wage requirements. Under temporary contract programs (Contracts ANAPEC) designed to help new entrants into the job market, the government pays social security and medical insurance contributions for the employee, and employers are required to pay above the minimum wage and hire 60 percent of ANAPEC interns at the conclusion of the contract. Contracts ANAPEC, however, fell outside the jurisdiction of the labor code and thus could be abused.

The law provides for a 44- to 48-hour maximum workweek with no more than 10 hours in a single day, premium pay for overtime, paid public and annual holidays, and minimum conditions for health and safety, including a prohibition on night work for women and minors. The law prohibits excessive overtime.

Occupational health and safety standards, reviewed and enforced by the Ministry of Employment and Social Affairs, are rudimentary, except for a prohibition on the employment of women and children in certain dangerous occupations. The law prohibits persons under the age of 18 years old from hazardous work in 33 areas, including working in mines, handling dangerous materials, transporting explosives, and operating heavy machinery.

Many employers did not observe the legal provisions for conditions of work. The government did not effectively enforce basic provisions of the labor code, such as payment of the minimum wage and other basic benefits under the National Social Security Fund. The country's 409 labor inspectors attempted to monitor working conditions and investigate accidents, but lack of resources prevented effective enforcement of labor laws. Penalties were generally not sufficient to deter violations. Labor inspectors are also tasked with mediation of disputes, which competed with proactive inspection of worksites for compliance with labor laws.

According to NGOs, no major workplace accidents occurred during the year. There were, however, numerous media reports of accidents, sometimes fatal, on construction sites that had substandard standards or lacked safety equipment. In the formal sector, workers can remove themselves from situations that endangered health or safety without jeopardy to their employment, and authorities effectively protected employees in this situation.